HARMON

A Journey Toward Self Care

DR. TONI G. ALVARADO

FORWARD WRITTEN BY DR. SHAWNA WOODRUFF

Published By:
Dr. Toni G. Alvarado

www.drtonialvarado.com

Copyright ©2018
All rights reserved.

No part of this publication may be reproduced, stored in or introduced into a retrieval system or transmitted, in any form, or by any means (electronic, mechanical, photocopying, recording or otherwise), without the written permission of the author.

Book Design & Production by:
Custom Made For You graphic design studio
(770) 923-8783
www.custommadeforyou.net

ISBN: 978-0-9826487-2-8

Harmonize Your Life:
A Journey Toward Self-Care

This book is dedicated to all the women who, like me, have become proficient at juggling family, business, ministry, work, personal aspirations, dreams, and goals, and determined not to lose yourself in the process...

Victoria,
Peace & Harmony
Come to you
Dr. Jo A.
04/14/18

Many are asking how can we "balance it all." I am convinced that this is the wrong approach. Balance implies that everything is equal. Trying to make everything equal and giving all things the same level of urgency creates unhealthy practices. Dr. Antoinette Alvarado offers a better approach. Instead of seeking balance, she encourages us to blend our lives and seek harmony. In so doing, we will find freedom and peace.

Tina Flowers, Esq.
Winston Salem, NC.

In Harmonize Your Life: A Journey Toward Self-Care, the reader is challenged to face personal realities. Dr. Toni's transparency about her own experiences forces the reader to look within and consider what is important and what is not in his or her own life. She nudges us right up to the doorway of a better, healthier life, but makes it clear that we must make the choice to walk through the door. As we consider Dr. Toni's suggestions, we can look forward to the harmony and rhythm that makes life melodious.

The Reverend Dr. Sabrina J. Ellis
Pentecostal Church of Christ
Cleveland, OH

"Harmony" and balance are words that seem to allude and escape those of us who are in ministry and who are always multi-tasking. At some point we must stop and evaluate what we are doing and make a concerted effort to change. This must needed book my Dr. Alvarado gives us some practical ways in which we can accomplish both." The genius of the book is the author is not writing from theory, this is her reality. I have known her for many years and I have watched her as she has learned to engage in self-care.

Rev. Dr. Jessica Kendall Ingram
Episcopal Supervisor
1st District African Methodist Episcopal Church

Fitness training is important for women because they lose calcium and hormones as they grow older. Exercise slows down the aging process, improves mental capacity, aids in the management of stress and an overall gift to yourself. Dr. Toni Alvarado is an ambitious and motivated client who motivates other clients in the gym. Because of her determination, focus, and positive attitude she has achieved major results. Dr. Toni has written this practical book in hopes of motivating her readers to embrace a lifestyle of fitness that produces Harmony.

Gabel Sims, Fitness Trainer
Temple Builder, Inc.
Atlanta, GA

An Invitation to the Journey

Self-Care has been a personal value for many years. Yet, I find it difficult to maintain a lifestyle of self-care without degrees of focus and intentionality. As professional men and women, entrepreneurs, parents, pastors, students and family members we function in so many roles that we often find ourselves running on empty with our emotional, mental, physical and spiritual tanks depleted at the end of a calendar year. Many people report that they are over-committed and fight feelings of guilt when saying "No" to the unrealistic expectations of people. Some report out-of-control schedules and lack of energy due to life and work demands. Others report a lack of personal motivation for self-care practices such as healthy eating, exercise, play and rest. The relentless busyness of western culture gives little space to reflect, refresh, re-focus, and re-energize with each phase of life. The truth is, many people can relate to the struggle of creating balance in their daily lives while pursuing their dreams. Therefore, consider this your personal invitation to journey with me and discover strategies for maintaining a lifestyle of harmony through a systematic approach to self-care.

Forever on the journey with you,

Dr. Toni G. Alvarado

Dr. Shawna Woodruff
Biography

Dr. Shawna Woodruff is a national board certified family wellness chiropractor, certified nutrition response testing practitioner, reiki master, and certified womb sauna practitioner. She is the owner and founder of Conyers Holistic Chiropractic & Nutrition, a holistic wellness center located in Conyers, Georgia. Her practice follows the philosophy: Brain, Body, Spine Family Wellness and provides a multitude of services which help re-organize and re-train the body in the key areas which directly affect an individual's overall wellbeing (Personal Development Life Coaching, Nutrition Response Testing, and Gentle Chiropractic Care). Dr. Woodruff works with individuals, families, small businesses, and corporate companies looking to improve and maintain their current state of health naturally.

FOREWARD
by Dr. Shawna Woodruff

"An illness of the body is always the outer expression and translation of a disorder, a disharmony in the inner being"
– The Mother

Many people assume that health is only the absence of disease; however, if you think about it, several of the most common deadly diseases appear in what seems to be silence. Imagine if you were so conscious, so elevated and so in tune with your body that you knew exactly the moment that something changed; exactly the moment that disharmony occurred and sickness entered your body. Would that not be amazing? What if I told you that this was possible? What if I told you that when you are in harmony in all areas of your (mind, body, spirit), the state of your overall health is more likely to be revealed to you? Would you be interested in knowing how to live with such awareness? Many of the things in our lives that are expressed outside of us are a direct reflection of either the harmony or disharmony within us.

Your overall health and harmony is a lifelong effort of consciousness. It is not something that just happens, instead it is something that you remain aware of and consistently put thought and effort towards improving and maintaining. It is work, and it takes a team, or as Dr. Toni discusses in the following pages, a "self-care board of directors". This is the team that aids in the management of your conscious awareness of the state of your mind, body and spirit. You are the president and CEO of that board, and it is up to you to implement and delegate the other director's positions along your journey. Besides, harmony is not a destination – it is indeed a journey.

If you're anything like me, you work hard for everything you have and in everything that you do. You choose to put your blood, sweat, tears and heart into everything you touch because you know it will be a reflection of you. Although these are wonderful attributes to have, in order for us to do these things at our greatest capacity, we must be in harmony. When we are in harmony, we produce our best work and we represent our best self. As a doctor, I spend every day caring for the health and wellness of all of my patients, many weeks seeing over 100 patients in just a few days. It wasn't until I entered my fourth year in private practice that I understood that giving from an empty cup would surely leave me depleted before I would be able to celebrate the victory of my fifth year milestone of successful practice. I began to be tired, frustrated, restless, sick, and at times I literally just wanted to quit! What I quickly realized was that in order to serve others, I had to first serve myself. I had to put my mask on first!

My hips ached at the end of my day, migraine headaches woke me up in the middle of the night, and my womb screamed at me during my menstrual cycle. It was time that I began diligently practicing all of the things that I had for several years taught my patients. I began consulting with a mentor about my future plans in practice so that I would become more organized in my thinking.

I scheduled weekly massages to help rid myself of tired and aching muscles and joints from working such long hours seeing patients. I purchased highly recommended inspirational books to begin reading daily to keep my spirit fed. I bought a new journal and began to write as much as possible to purge myself of the day's matters. I spent quiet time to myself to calm my mind, reconnect and re-center. I received a nutrition response testing health check to find out what vitamins and minerals my body needed to function better, and began taking them. I committed to a gym membership, found a group of workout partners to help hold me accountable and scheduled days that I would spend time focusing on cardio, flexibility and strength.

I had a conversation with my womb (yes I spoke to myself) and inwardly reflected while asking ways had I neglected her, and how I could make things better. I even adopted a vegan lifestyle and started to pay attention to what I was putting in my body and on my body. Lastly, but surely not least, I went back to what I knew was the center of all things in my life since I was a little girl, I became intentional about my relationship with God.

The way our bodies work, we cannot fixate on one area that we want to harmonize and think that the other areas will just follow. We have to be intentional about every area: mind, body, and spirit and give each area effort. One of the major obstacles I have dealt with in my own life during periods of disharmony is remembering to think good thoughts. That may sound easy, but many of us battle with this simple rule of harmony. We create what we think. Having good thoughts contributes to your mindfulness, and mindfulness is directly correlated with specific signals that are imprinted in your brain and communicated throughout the rest of your body.

If your brain and body receives good thoughts and good signals, we are innately more in harmony – we are at a higher vibration. In addition to thinking good thoughts, you must be proactive instead of reactive. When you prepare yourself by becoming more organized in your lives, you are better positioned to adapt to any situation that you are confronted with. This in turn results in less overall stress. Less stress means more harmony!

Above all things, the greatest focus has to be your conscious decision to bring attention to the areas that aid in bringing harmony into your life. You can read all of the self-help books on the shelves, consult with all of your "self-care board of directors", and you can go through this book and understand every single word but if you do not make the conscious decision to change and begin to do the work required, the journey will in fact be a lot more difficult.

I challenge you to think good thoughts, begin writing those thoughts down and place them where you can consistently see them and read them, consult with your "self-care board of directors", and tell everyone that believes in you and supports you about your good thoughts. Be in alignment every single day and you will see that the universe is on your side.

After personally shedding over 40 pounds of excess weight, stress, and disorganization life has been a lot more harmonized for me. I am happier and feel more accomplished that I ever have! I am able to think more clearly, make better decisions for myself and my future, I am more productive, my work is a direct reflection and expression of my harmony, my relationships with others has greatly improved, and those around me truly have noticed that so many things about me have changed! My life has elevated. I have evolved and everything about me speaks harmony. Join the journey to greater harmony. I promise that it will be one that will be something that will provide clarity and understanding of your purpose. Harmony awaits you. All you have to do is do the work and claim it!

Always aim at complete harmony of thought and word and deed…. and everything will be well.
~ Mahatma Gandhi

Harmony Vs. Balance

Life is like a score of music, with simultaneous combinations of tones and rhythms. Our lives can be lived in a manner that makes the chaos of our lives come together in harmonious rhythms. These harmonious rhythms are unique to who we are and what we are called to do. Like a musical score, when blended together into the right chordal structure, life becomes a melodic masterpiece that is pleasing to the ear.

Since life happens simultaneously, we live, work and play within the same life span. Therefore, we must discover ways to blend the various parts of our lives into a euphonious structure of chords that flow congruently into a symphonic lifestyle. Just like the score of music determines the notes, rhythms, rest points, moods, feelings and crescendos of a musical masterpiece, our lives can be conducted in a mode that gives room to each movement of life. Each movement must be done at the right moments, in the right places, with the right people in harmony with our purpose.

For many years I sought to strike a healthy balance between marriage, family, work and personal pursuits. I'm often asked the infamous "balance" question, "How do you balance all of the things you do? You're a wife, mother, pastor, CEO of a non-profit organization, college professor, coach, businesswoman, itinerant preacher, and international speaker. How in the world do you do it?" My response to that question heretofore has been the typical balance response of making sure I have good time management and a good team of people around me to aid in all of my responsibilities. I give much credence to having a good wellness plan to keep myself holistically healthy. I agree that good time management, good support teams and wellness plans are necessary to live a "balanced" lifestyle. Yet, I too find myself asking the balance question. I have taught seminars and workshops entitled The Balancing Act, only to struggle with the elusive ideal of balancing my own life.

The word balance suggests that we are in a constant state of equilibrium with an equal distribution of weight and tension. However, life is not easily packaged in equal amounts of experiences and responsibilities. In fact, we are always in a state of flux trying to decide what amount of attention to give to the various aspects of our lives. The challenge with balance is that it is a moving target and just when I think I have mastered it, the target moves and I have to make the right decision for the present moment and current life issue that I am facing.

After years of being worn out from my quest for balance, I am positing a new word to shift the conversation in the direction of something more attainable for those who manage multiple passions. I am breaking free from the ideal of maintaining balance and asserting the word harmony, a far more attainable virtue to maintain in my life. Just hearing the word harmony brings a sense of peace and tranquility to my mind, body and spirit. It causes me to exhale and breathe in new life. Harmony suggests that I can bring the different parts of my life together into consistent orderly agreement and practical congruity.

In the following chapters I will elaborate on self-care principles, skills, and strategies that are sure to help us maintain harmony in our lives. Much of what I will share are life lessons from my personal quest for harmony. I will share information and wisdom I have gleaned from expert psychologists, psychiatrists, physicians, pastors and priests. Finally, I will share from my experiences with the people I call my "self-care board of directors." These are health and wellness professionals, coaches, mentors, fitness trainers, family and friends to whom I have made myself accountable.

I must warn you, harmony is not an easy virtue to acquire and maintain. It will require a renovation of your attitude, habits and may alter or redefine some of your closest relationships. Ready? Harmony trumps balance, I'm going for harmony in my life. Hopefully you will too.

Coaching Moment:
What needs to come into complete harmony in your life? Why?

_____
_____
_____
_____
_____
_____
_____
_____

*I think self-awareness is probably
the most important thing towards being a champion.*
~ Billie Jean King

*The better awareness, the better your choices.
As you make better choices, you will
see better results.*
~ Anonymous

Self-Awareness Is Essential

Self-awareness is a psychological state in which people are aware of their traits, feelings and behaviors. It is defined as a realization of oneself as an individual entity. This awareness does not mean that the individual is separate from the whole. Self-awareness occurs the moment we take notice of ourselves in a situation or in connection within a larger system of people. Self-awareness emerges at different points of the life cycle. This can happen in early childhood, adolescence, adulthood, mid-life, or senior life.

Self-awareness is having a clear perspective of our unique call and design. It provides clarity concerning who and what we are called to be and do. It also provides clarity concerning what and who we are not called to be and do. It is a clear perspective of our personality traits, strengths, weaknesses, beliefs, emotions, motivations and values. Self-awareness requires an acceptance of who we are with all of our gifts, skills, and growth opportunities.

For many years, I suffered with low self-esteem, not valuing myself because my dark skin tone did not fit the image of what I was socialized to view as attractive. I learned to value myself through a process of identity formation, spiritual transformation and the development of authentic relationships with a cadre of family, friends, and female mentors. This process led to an emotional, psychological and spiritual awakening that resulted in healthy self-esteem. I discovered that I could not truly value others until I fully embraced the masterpiece I am created to be, and discover what I am created to do. The self-awareness process with coaches and mentors proved valuable in gaining greater clarity about myself. As I increased my level of self-awareness, I gained inspiration to make necessary changes in my life.

Coaching Moment:
Self-awareness is the first step toward living a life of harmony. Do some soul searching on the things that are unique about you, such as your gifts, skills, abilities and passions. Match those things to the activities, jobs and opportunities that are consistent with who you are and what is important to you. Once you have reflected, journal about it here:

_____
_____
_____
_____
_____
_____
_____
_____
_____
_____
_____
_____
_____

The best investment you can make is in yourself. Self-care, self-love and self-development. Give more to yourself and you will have more to give to others.
~ Akiroq Brost

When you recover or discover something that nourishes your soul and brings joy, care enough about yourself to make room for it in your life.
~ Jean Shinoda Bolen

Place Your Own Mask On First!

Self-care is vital in order to manage all that has been entrusted to our care. We cannot properly care for the people in our lives, if we are not attending to our emotional, mental, physical and spiritual care. In my first book *Run & Not Be Weary: The Pursuit of Purpose and Destiny*, I candidly share how self-care became a lived value. It was through a process of suffering from burnout that ultimately led to a hyper-thyroid condition that awakened me to my need for self-care. I discovered that self-care is required if I am to maximize my capacity to coach, pastor, preach, teach and pursue every opportunity afforded to me.

On my 37th birthday my husband asked what I desired as a birthday gift. I exhaustively replied, "A treadmill." Our oldest son Johnathan, II was 2 years old, our younger son Joshua was 14 months, and our daughter, Ariel was 8 months at that time. We were parenting three children under age 3 and I was trying to be "super-mom."

In addition to my responsibilities at home, our local church was in a season of rapid growth. We were facilitating multiple Sunday worship services in multiple locations, television ministry and an extensive itinerant preaching ministry. To add to that pressure, my husband and I were enrolled in seminary pursuing the Master of Divinity Degree. We were driving 2 hours, each way, to and from Atlanta, Georgia to Cleveland, Tennessee, 2-3 times a week depending on our course load. I was desperately trying to balance family, ministry, school and work. It was not long before I became physically tired, emotionally drained, spiritually arid, and rapidly moving toward burnout.

I noticed that I was having racing thoughts and could not remain focused. My hands would shake so bad; I could barely hold a pen to write. My heart would palpitate so fast that I could feel my heart beating on the bed whenever I laid down to rest or sleep. After consulting with my primary physician, I was referred to an endocrinologist who diagnosed me with Graves' Disease, a condition of the thyroid that results in an over-active thyroid. Graves' Disease can be fatal if not treated properly. I was advised that Grave's Disease is incurable, but if treated properly with medication could go into remission.

When I surveyed my life, I discovered that I was doing a good job of taking care of everyone and a poor job of caring for myself. I suddenly realized that I was often last on my "to-do list" if I made the list at all. I began asking serious internal questions such as, "Why am I doing all of these things? Why do I feel the need to perform? Why am I afraid of saying no? What am I really gaining from all of this busyness? What things do I need to take off of my plate? What things can I delegate?" I thought about my family and began envisioning their lives without me. I began asking myself questions such as, "Who will raise my children if I die prematurely? Who will my husband marry, if something happens to me? Who is going to enjoy the life we built together if I die before enjoying the fruit of our labor?"

At this critical juncture, I began to desire a deeper life of harmony. I started where I was at the time. I purchased a treadmill, joined my local YMCA and began a moderate exercise program. I hired a personal trainer and began my journey toward self-care. I began enjoying the notion that I could take care of myself while taking care of others.

I made a conscious decision to eliminate the stressors I had begun to accommodate. I developed a regiment of healthy eating, exercise, rest and relaxation. In addition to these strategies, I began educating myself by reading and taking counsel with fitness coaches, nutritionists, health and wellness professionals. I trained my mind and body to eat healthy, drink water and abandon unhealthy habits that I had developed all of my life.

I hired a life coach to assist me in developing strategies for managing my busy life. Our sessions were filled with questions that prompted me to develop better self-care skills, release control and delegate. I had to confront my fear of loss and rejection that drove me to perform for acceptance. My coaching sessions were filled with tears as my coach held me accountable to confronting my fears and developing a healthier lifestyle. I discovered that I am enough. I do not have to perform for acceptance and self-care is a must if I am to maintain a life of harmony.

When I think of self-care I am reminded of those infamous words spoken by flight attendants during the safety presentation on every flight: "In the event of an emergency, an oxygen mask will descend. Place your own mask on first before attempting to help those who are seated around you." One might ask what motivates me to consistently get up for those early morning workouts, eat healthy, rest and rejuvenate your mind, body and spirit. The answer is quite simple, I'm Placing My Own Mask On First!

Coaching Moment:
Reflect on the following questions and write your answers here: What critical juncture are you facing in your life right now? What will happen if you ignore your signs of burnout? What does it mean for you to put on your own mask first?

Living in a way that reflects one's values is not just about what you do, it is also about how you do things.
~ Deborah Day

*When your values are clear to you,
making decisions
becomes easier.*
~ Roy Disney

Self-Care Is About Values

Core values serve as the the compass that guides our thoughts and actions. When brought to our conscious awareness, core values shed light on our behavior and habits. A value is a principle, standard or a quality that is considered worthwhile or desirable. Without core values our lives are devoid of meaning and purpose. When we are properly aligned with our core values, we live meaningful and purposeful lives.

Values can range from the commonplace, such as the belief in hard work and punctuality, to the more psychological, such as self-reliance, concern for others, and harmony of purpose. Our values are the building blocks of our thought patterns. Our thoughts are the building blocks of our actions. Our actions are the building blocks of our lifestyle. Thus our behavior and habits are the visible expression of what we deem as important, true and valuable.

We can revitalize our lives by making an effort to implement the values to which we aspire. Implementing our values energizes us toward the fulfillment of our dreams, goals and visions. Committing to and applying healthy values helps us to achieve success and well-being. Therefore, our values are reinforced by the lifestyle we choose to live.

In a conversation with one of my coaches, I was asked the question, "What patterns do you see in your life that reflect your value for self-care?" She challenged me to think through my self-care value and assisted me in the development of what I now call my "Self-Care Practices." This list includes a variety of health and wellness activities such as: physical exercise, healthy eating, rest, family time, vacations, prayer, reading, spa visits, retreats, facials, massages, self-development seminars and conferences (where I am not facilitating or speaking), fun and laughter with my family and friends. My self-care practices are aligned with my values for family, personal development, peace, tranquility, emotional, physical and spiritual vitality.

As a result of this intentional process, self-care moved from being an aspirational value, something that I admired in others, to an actual value that is demonstrated through a diverse set of healthy practices that are lived on a daily, weekly, monthly and annual basis. My self-care practices are unique to my personality, temperament, life structure, passions and desires. My self-care list changes, and morphs with me. I may emphasize a specific practice at a particular season and emphasize another practice during another season of my life. The key is to discover what rejuvenates me and remain committed to my values for self-care.

Coaching Moment:
Reflect on your self-care values and match each value to a self-care practice. For example:

My Self-Care Value	My Self-Care Practice
Peace & Tranquility	Regular visits to the spa and The Monastery of The Holy Spirit.
Family Time	Family meals, recreation and family vacations.

In the table below create your self-care values and self-care practice list.

My Self-Care Value	My Self-Care Practice

Coaching Moment:

Coaching Moment:

As you remove toxic people from your life, you free up space and emotional energy for positive, healthy relationships.
~ John Mark Green

Relationships with anyone are at their best when you are at your best.
~ Maria Dorfner

Cultivate Healthy Relationships

Relationships make our lives worth living and can be a source of personal fulfillment. However, relationships do not always develop in healthy and mutually satisfying directions making unhealthy relationships a source of discontentment and disharmony. Harmonizing our lives requires that we maintain healthy relationships with family, friends, colleagues, co-workers, and significant others.

Healthy relationship skills must be learned if we are to maintain healthy relationships. Conflict resolution is a critical relationship skill that produces harmony. In order to resolve conflict both parties must agree on the source of the problem, a time to talk about the problem and reasonable time-frame for resolving the problem. Mutual respect must characterize the conversation when talking through conflict. Both parties must remain calm, open and positive concerning conflict resolution. Be flexible and have at least two options you can live with while working toward a win-win solution.

Healthy Communication is another critical relationship skill. One must communicate forthrightly and take ownership for their feelings and beliefs, using words such as "I believe… I feel… I would like… I have decided." Practice speaking to those who have hurt you in a manner that expresses how their actions have impacted you. For example: When you… I feel

… Remember healthy communication requires listening for meaning and understanding which requires that we go deeper than listening on a surface level.

Practicing forgiveness is an essential relationship skill that produces harmony in our lives. We must learn to forgive the offenses of others and prevent feelings of bitterness that can fester in the mind, soul and psyche. Letting go requires that we release people from past hurts, unrealistic expectations and will free us to focus on healthy relationships. Getting the necessary counsel with family, friends, psychiatrists or therapist can help you resolve relational disappointment, injury and pain. Remember, "He who cannot forgive another breaks the bridge over which he must pass himself." ~ George Herbert

Coaching Moment:

Evaluate your relationship with a friend, spouse, co-worker, child, sibling or family member. Ask yourself some key questions:

Is This Relationship Nourishing?
- Does this person express appreciation for my contribution to the relationship?
- Do I sense that this person enjoys being with me?
- Do I feel at ease when I am with this person?
- Do I believe this person considers me a positive influence in his/her life?
- Do I believe there is a realistic balance between the efforts I put into this relationship and the rewards I experience?

Is This Relationship Toxic?

- Does this person often criticize me?
- Do I find that this person talks more about my mistakes than my accomplishments?
- Does this person frequently lose his/her temper with me?
- Does this person often yell at me?
- Does this person put me down in the presence of others?
- Is this relationship defined as abusive, controlling, manipulative or unethical?

If the relationship you just reflected upon is malnourishing or toxic, here is an opportunity to harmonize your life by re-defining the relationship.

Answer the following questions in the space below:

Does pain, fear or distrust dominates the relationship? Do you need to re-evaluate this relationship? What corrective measures need to be implemented to bring this relationship into harmony?

*It's how we spend our time here and now,
that really matters. If you are fed up with the way
you have come to interact with time, change it.*
~ Marcia Wieder

If you want to make good use of your time, you've got to know what's most important and then give it all you've got.
~ Lee Iacocca

Manage Your Time

Time is one of our most precious commodities. When we manage our time we create a harmonious flow of tasks that are consistent with our priorities for each specific day. Effective time management relieves us from the need to move hurriedly throughout the day. It is not about marking off accomplished tasks from our "to-do list". In fact, effective time management may require that we do less in a 24-hour day.
Time management requires that we set priorities for our lives. Priorities must be set on a macro and micro level. Macro priorities determine the activities, people and organizations we devote our time long-term. Micro priorities determine the daily and weekly tasks that support our long-term goals, plans and vision.

Time management requires one of three approaches: finding time, taking time or making time.[1] Finding time means I use whatever time that is available or created for me by others. It is much like a scavenger hunt where I am turning over tasks and assignments looking for "me-time."

Taking time is similar to finding time. Taking time means I am borrowing time from other tasks. People who allocate

---

[1] Linda Clark. Leadership Essentials for Women. Birmingham, AL: New Hope Publishers, 2004, 139-140.

time this way are always over-committed, overextended and overwhelmed. They never evaluate their activities and determine whether or not they should be involved in a particular event, program or project.

The antithesis to finding and taking time, is making time. Making time is an intentional planning and deciding of the way time is allocated and budgeted. Making time requires thoughtful preparation and purposeful decision making on how I will spend my time. This allows me to weigh each opportunity against my purpose and eliminates the tendency to make decisions based upon the opinions of others.

Coaching Moment:

Evaluate your time based upon the following reflection questions and write about it here:

1. Does your life feel out of control? If so, in what areas?

_____
_____
_____
_____
_____
_____

2. Are you more of a time-taker, time-finder, or time-maker?

_____
_____
_____
_____
_____
_____

3. What can you do to become a time-maker?

_____
_____
_____
_____
_____
_____
_____

To feel more fulfilled your actions and activities need to be in alignment with what you deem important.
~ Deborah Day

One is often so busy doing life that is easy to avoid evaluating whether you are putting your energy in the direction you value most.
~ Deborah Day

Separate the Urgent from the Important

One of my favorite household chores is laundry. I enjoy the aroma of laundry detergent, fabric softener and the warmth of clothes being pulled from the dryer. As a young girl, my mother taught me to separate clothes that are full of bright and dark colors from the white clothes. It only took one time for me to discover that neglecting this important laundry technique would result in clothes that are discolored and altered forever. Likewise, we must learn to separate the urgent from the important if we are to maintain a life of harmony.

Everything that is urgent is not important. Yet, many people struggle with deciding what is important and what is urgent. There is a constant tension between the urgent and what is really important. Overly attending to the urgent is often at the expense of the important and can result in a negative impact. If we are not careful, the urgent will overshadow the important resulting in negligence of self-care, an arid spiritual life, quality time with family and friends, and an abandonment of important tasks at home and work.

We must become comfortable living in the tension of the urgent and important and choose what is most expedient. An inability to separate the urgent from the important can be linked to improper boundaries with family and friends. This is often the case when we allow the poor planning of others to encroach upon our time or we feel the need to directly respond to every situation that comes into our path.

Coaching Moment:

Separating the urgent from the important produces greater levels of harmony, peace and tranquility. If you are one of those people who struggle with separating the urgent from the important consider reflecting on your priorities, taking a personal inventory of your time, asking yourself will this matter in ten years and writing your thoughts here:

_____
_____
_____
_____
_____
_____
_____
_____
_____
_____
_____
_____
_____
_____
_____
_____
_____
_____
_____
_____
_____
_____
_____
_____

By saying yes, when we really wish we could just say no, we are giving our time and energy away.
~ Angie Johnsey

People think focus means saying yes to the thing you've got to focus on. But that's not what it means at all. It means saying no to the hundred other good ideas that are there. You have to pick carefully. I'm actually as proud of the the things we haven't done as the things I have done. Innovation is saying no to 1,000 things.
~ Steve Jobs

Never Say Yes in The Moment

Over the years, I have learned not to say yes, in the moment. Whenever I say yes without consulting with my calendar and previous commitments, I find myself over-committed and overwhelmed. Things flow better when I thank the person making the request for thinking of me, and respond to their request after I have consulted with my calendar and previous commitments.

One of the most liberating feelings is when I learned that I did not have to say yes to every request made of me. I have learned that when I say yes to something, I am actually saying no to something else. Therefore, I make every effort to weigh my decisions against, my purpose, gifting and interest. In fact, whenever I circumvent this process, I pay for it in time, money, energy and sometimes relationally.

There are many reasons why people struggle with the common problem of saying no. Linda Clark shares the common reasons why people have problems saying no: [2]

1. We want to gain the approval and acceptance of others.

---

[2] Linda Clark. Leadership Essentials for Women; 148.

2. We are afraid of offending friends and acquaintances.
3. We feel guilty for not measuring up to someone else's standards.
4. We are busy makes me feel important.
5. We link over-commitment with my spirituality.
6. We agree because of low self-esteem.
7. We have a compelling need to be needed by others.

Whenever our yes leads to over-commitment, it will eventually lead to stress, burnout and poor health. Some may find their joy ultimately turns into resentment of the persons and tasks to whom they are saying yes. Many people feel unsuccessful when they are agreeing to projects that are not consistent with their skill-set, passion and purpose. Therefore, saying yes when we should say no often leads to an unfocused life filled with distractions, frustrations and unfulfilled dreams.

Coaching Moment:

Linda Clark gives effective guidelines for breaking the yes habit. Review the list below, check the guideline that you need to embrace. Write a plan for using this guideline to help you break the yes habit.

1. Think before you say yes. Evaluate your motives and determine why you are saying yes.
2. Prioritize, Pray and seek God's will.
3. Ask. "What will this cost me in time, effort, money, relationships and progress toward my goals?"
4. Consult your calendar, asking how this fits with your other plans and responsibilities.
5. Communicate to ensure others are aware of your time demands.
6. Don't let others establish your priorities.
7. Don't be a "solve it all", a chronic "fixer", or "control freak".
8. Remember someone else's time problems are not your responsibility.

*There is no such thing as Superwoman.
You can't have everything if you do everything.
~ Gloria Steinem*

> "A Superwoman isn't a woman who can do anything, but a woman who avoids doing too much."
> ~Shirley Conran

Overcome the Superwoman Syndrome

One of the reasons we do not engage in self-care practices is because we have bought into the superwoman syndrome. We think we can leap tall buildings in a single bound and save everybody in our world. The truth is, we are human, we get tired and we do not possess inexhaustible time and energy. We do not have to be strong all of the time and we can allow people to see our inconsistencies. We can admit that we are vulnerable to our personal kryptonite and sometimes our cape is tattered and torn.

Unfortunately, I learned this lesson after being diagnosed with Grave's Disease (hyper-thyroid condition). I was suddenly confronted with my own superwoman syndrome. I took great pride in being the best wife, mother and pastor in the world only to discover my own weaknesses. I suddenly had to learn how to ask for help, delegate and confront the false sense of pride that came with all of my roles and responsibilities.

Learning how to delegate is essential to overcoming the superwoman syndrome. To do so we must relinquish control and the fear of losing authority. Delegating does not mean that we relinquish total responsibility or credit for a job well done. It gives room for team members to grow and experience success. In fact, when we delegate, the entire team benefits from the success of individual members.

Delegating is not an admission of failure or inadequacy. It frees us to dedicate our time to the relationships and responsibilities that are significant to our life goals and mission. Delegating relieves us of the stress of being super and grants us permission to be totally human.

Coaching Moment:

Examine reasons why you don't delegate by checking the list below:
- I think if I don't do it, no one will.
- I think I am the best person for the job.
- I am afraid of losing control.
- I enjoy getting the credit for a job well done.
- I am afraid of admitting that I cannot do it.
- I think delegating is an admission of failure.
- I don't like to ask for help.
- I delegated in the past and it did not go well.
- It takes too much time to teach someone how to do it.
- Other reasons that are not listed above:

_____
_____
_____

Which of the delegating tips below do you need to embrace?
- Trust the people on my team.
- Believe in other people's ability to get it done.
- Relinquish control.
- Praise other people for a job well done.
- Delegate the things that I cannot do.
- Ask for help.
- Get over past experiences.
- Train other people on the team.
- Other delegating tips that are not listed above.

_____
_____
_____

You don't need a holistic cure you need a holistic lifestyle. Look after yourself in every way, mind, body, and soul.
~ Akiroq Brost

When we give ourselves compassion, we are opening our hearts in a way that can transform our lives.
~ Kristin Neff

Live Holistically

As a Christian woman I believe God requires me to live a life of wholeness, spirit, soul and body. Over the years, life and work can have negative effects our spiritual, emotional, mental and physical health. We live with family dysfunctions, personal disappointments, rejections and fears, toxic relationships and environments that can result in impoverished mental and physical realities. Therefore, self-care must be practiced holistically to address all of life, spiritually, emotionally and physically.

Wayne Muller states, In this relentless busyness of modern life, we have lost the rhythm between work and rest.[4] When we are dealing with the demands of spouses, children, jobs, challenging family members and friends, tight schedules, questionable finances, and personal dreams and goals, stress and anxiety can become the norm in our lives. We are killing ourselves trying to be obedient to self-imposed expectations and societal stereotypes. We give imbalanced attention to the public life at the expense of the private.[5] Therefore, we become involved in more meetings and programs to gain personal fulfillment. Our massive responsibilities at home, work, and church have resulted in a lot of good people on the verge of collapse.[6]

---

[4] Wayne Muller. Sabbath: Finding Rest, Renewal and Delight in Our Daily Lives. New York, NY: Bantam Books, 1999, 1.

[5] Gordon MacDonald. Ordering Your Private World. Nashville, TN: Thomas Nelson, Inc. 2003, 7.

[6] Gordon MacDonald. Ordering Your Private World; 6.

Spiritual Care

Spiritual wholeness requires that we pay attention to our spiritual being as the anchor for existence. Spiritual anemia sets in when we neglect the inner self and personal relationship with God. People who practice self-care are intentional about the care of their spiritual life.

Emotional Care

Emotional wholeness is connected to spiritual wholeness. Acquiring and maintaining healthy spirituality is part of "good" self-care. Many people have ignored insecurities, deceptions that lie at the core of their emotional, sexual and physical dysfunctions. People who are emotionally imbalanced tend to over spiritualize, cover hurts, brokenness and grief with spiritual pretense.[7] Emotionally drained people will often depend on material things and participate in obsessive compulsive behaviors such as over-eating and shopping as a coping mechanism. Emotionally healthy people become open, honest and vulnerable to those who can help them heal emotional wounds and eliminate patterns of self-destructive behavior and thinking.

Physical Care

Good physical health is connected to spiritual and emotional health. Many times we have not emphasized the importance of our bodies in connection to our goals, dreams, visions and overall life purpose. Statistics have shown that many professionals and high stressed careers such as pastors, politicians, college presidents, policemen and women are negligent in the area of self-care. Many diseases are associated with poor nu-

---

[7]Peter Scazzero. The Emotionally Healthy Church. Grand Rapids, MI: Zondervan, 2003, 74-75.

trition, lack of exercise, stress, mental and physical overloads. Lack of commitment to one's physical care can lead to apathy and burn out. To combat this epidemic in our contemporary culture we must develop a network of health providers, physical and nutritional education to improve your overall physical health. Additionally, we must develop a realistic routine for exercise and proper diet of which I will unpack more in later chapters.

Coaching Moment:
Which area of holistic living are you needing to be more intentional in your practice of self-care? Spiritual, Emotional, Physical? Why? How do you plan to be more intentional in these areas of self-care?

_____
_____
_____
_____
_____
_____
_____
_____
_____
_____
_____
_____
_____
_____
_____
_____

For me, fitness is not just about hitting the gym; it is also about an inner happiness and an overall well-being.
~ Rakul Preet Singh

Take care of your body. It's the only place you have to live.
~ Jim Rohn

#Fitness Motivation

Several years ago I decided to increase my level of fitness. I have taken different approaches by trying new sports and participating in fitness classes that I once avoided. One of the fitness classes that I use to dread was spin. Admittedly, I attended a spin class many years ago and vowed that I would never do it again. Because of that experience (that I did not enjoy), I convinced myself that this activity was not designed for me. After years of watching others go in and out of spin classes excited about their experience, I finally mustered up enough courage to try it again. I'm happy to say, I conquered my fear of spin and it is now a class that I truly enjoy.

In addition to spin, I have enjoyed kickboxing, strength training and yoga classes. I enjoy bike riding in my favorite parks and because I live in Georgia, hiking, running and walking at Stone Mountain Park has become one of my favorite routines. While it is challenging, I enjoy every moment of of my fitness journey.

Whether, I am training with fitness a coach, a fitness camp or on my own, I actively post to social media to motivate others to stay fit. Because of the things I post about my own fitness journey, people have been inspired and many have started exercising due to my example. I wish I could boast that I never get tired or experience moments when I do not want to work out. It is not easy to get out of bed before dawn, especially when you manage a busy family and lifestyle such my own.

Over the years I have developed a thinking pattern that is vital to my fitness motivation. There are times during my workout when the routine is challenging and negative thoughts will prompt the desire to give up or quit. However, I have learned to lasso negative thoughts before they dominate my mind. One of my best practices is the recitation of scripture and self-care quotes that constantly encourage me to think positively and to remember my fitness goals.

Training your body requires that you train your mind. While working out, I focus my mind on the benefits of a healthy lifestyle and away from the temporary pain or struggle that I might be experiencing in the moment. When I view the workout as a necessary component to my overall health plan, I am able to make direct correlations between my thought patterns and my ability to accomplish the task at hand. Thinking positively about why I am exercising gives me the energy and strength that I need to finish well. Whether it is exercise, healthy eating, or accomplishing a fitness goal, how I think really affects my ability to get it done and remain motivated.

The world of fitness is vast there are many ways to engage in physical exercise. Here are some points to consider if you are just starting out on your fitness journey:

- Do what fits or works best for you.
- Do not be intimidated by what others do or enjoy.
- Do not compare yourself to others at school, work or the gym.
- Make sure the exercise routine that you choose is suitable for your age, height weight, fitness level or specific health concerns.

- Consult your physician.
- Hire a fitness coach, trainer or join a fitness group.
- DO NOT SIGN A LONG-TERM GYM MEMBERSHIP CONTRACT!
- Find a gym that will allow you to pay on a daily, monthly or 90-day plan.
- Walking is free! Find a nearby park or walking trail and start walking.
- Set realistic fitness goals for yourself.

Coaching Moment:
Describe your most recent exercise experience: What did you do? What did you enjoy about it? What did you not enjoy about it?

_____
_____
_____
_____
_____
_____
_____
_____

What would it take for you to engage in an exercise program (i.e. Finances, time, a coach, family support)?

_____
_____
_____
_____
_____
_____

Who can help you (i.e. A friend, a family, a family member, a workout partner, a fitness trainer)?

_____
_____
_____
_____
_____

Why is fitness important for you?

_____
_____
_____
_____
_____

When will you start? _____

_____
_____
_____
_____
_____
_____
_____
_____

Your beliefs affect your choices. Your choices shape your actions. Your actions determine your results.
~ Roy T. Bennett

Life is a matter of choices, and every choice you make makes you.
~John C. Maxwell

Choose Life

Life is a series of choices. In your lifetime you will make millions of choices great and small, good and bad. We are presented everyday with so many choices that making the right choice can overwhelm us at times. Some choices are so routine and automatic that we hardly think about them. Such as the choices to get out bed in the morning or the times that we will eat, sleep and play.

We make choices when we are driving, whether to switch lanes or take a different direction on the way home. Choices are all around us in our personal, professional and spiritual lives. In fact, God created us as free moral agents. Meaning, God gives us the freedom to choose where we will live, whom to love and the type of lifestyle we will live. God does not make our choices for us but requires that we manage the consequences of the choices we make.

Self-Care is a matter of consistency, commitment and choices. On a daily basis we are presented with choices that will either improve our lives or take our lives down a path of destruction. Just like those choices that we make on a daily basis, we can train our minds, bodies and spirits to make the right choices when confronted with temptation. Our lives are a sum total of the choices that we make.

In one biblical passage, Deuteronomy 30: 19. Moses is addressing the congregation of Israel about the choices that they will face on their pilgrimage through the wilderness. Moses is warning them of the dangers they will face on their journey and opportunities they will have to choose the wrong path. He not only cautions them regarding their choices but he helps them understand that the choices they make today will not only effect their lives but will have positive or negative impact on their children for generations to come. Moses gathers the people and challenges them with these words, "I have set before you, life and death, blessing and curse. Therefore, choose life, that you and your offspring may live."

I often think of this passage when I am engaging in self-care practices. In fact, if I fail to choose myself, I am failing to choose life. This is not a selfish practice, this is a practice that will sustain my life and sustain the lives of my children, husband, family, businesses, ministry and all who are assigned to me.

Coaching Moment:

Think about the choices you have made in recent years and rate the quality of those choices. What better choices do you need to make for your self-care?

_____
_____
_____
_____
_____
_____
_____
_____
_____
_____
_____
_____
_____
_____
_____
_____
_____
_____
_____
_____
_____
_____
_____

*An empty lantern provides no light.
Self-care is the fuel that allows your
light to shine brightly.*
~ Unknown

May the outward and inward be one.
~ Socrates

Go Inward

In his book, Ordering Your Private World, Gordon MacDonald writes out of thirst and desire to reflect on his own personal journey and his attempt to live a disciplined, focused, and effective inner life. MacDonald reports having had conversations with countless of men and women who are regretful and embarrassed about the amount of wasted time, abandoned goals, and lack of personal and spiritual growth that characterize their journey. He has encountered leaders who admit they lack the will or the personal organizing principles to actualize their highest hopes and dreams.

Too often we are too busy to tend to our personal private self and have confused this activity with the daily public activities that consume our thoughts and time. MacDonald states:

> "One of the great battlegrounds of the new century is within the private world of the individual. The values of our Western culture incline us to believe that the busy, publicly-active person in ministry is also the most spiritual. Tempted to give imbalanced attention to the public world at the expense of the private, we become involved in more programs, more meetings. Our massive responsibilities at home, work, and church have resulted in a lot of good people on the verge of collapse."[8]

[8]Gordon MacDonald. 5-6

When I discovered this I too had fallen into the trap of this Western culture it revolutionized my way of living and being in the world. I had to confront myself and make a deeper commitment to cultivate a rich inner life. Through my efforts I discovered that a fertile inner life is the secret to an effective public life.

Going Inward requires deliberate, intentional time that we dedicate to our inner life. Private fruitfulness produces increased competence and a sense of purposefulness to our public work. MacDonald reports that he was incessant in his work. His hours were filled with business meetings, people with problems, administrative details, speeches and talks that came one after another. He noticed that he was incessant, he never stopped, he was constantly going, his mood was what he described as "inky", he was having destabilizing thoughts and he was drained: spiritually, emotionally, intellectually, and physically[9] He assumed that energy and vitality were boundless and inexhaustible. He had unconsciously convinced himself that one could live at this furious pace forever and do it without any serious consequences.

This he did until his wife Gail, confronted him with his problem. One Saturday morning he sat at breakfast with his family trying to act interested and engaged, all the while, preoccupied with the stuff that lay ahead of him that day. The events of Sunday, was at the top of the pile, as he considered how he had to preach three times the next day and he had not taken the time to prepare. Gail, spoke up with a true and provocative observation "You've not spent much time with the children lately". In that moment MacDonald began to cry as he says "not a few tears and not for a short while."[10] He reports having cried for at least four hours. His wife dismissed the children and cancel the events of the day and held him in her arms as

[9]Gordon MacDonald. V-XVii

he cried like a baby over the sorrows that had been handed down from father to son from previous generations.

His focus was on large numbers, big bucks, sudden victories, quick recognition, and meeting "important people." His natural gifts, such as personal charisma, mental brightness, emotional strength, and organizational ability, was impressive and motivated people for a long time. The day he "hit the wall", he realized that these qualities had been mistaken for spiritual vitality and depth. MacDonald suggests that there are leaders who can build great organizations (including churches) on natural gifts. They can say the right words, exhibit keen insight, and connect with the right people for a long time without ever making the discovery that the inner life is close to empty.

MacDonald shares, "When we operate with such intentionality we will experience long-term fruitfulness, and our best years will be in the last half of our lives when discipline and depth will prove to be most valuable."[11] Like MacDonald we too must admit that we can be rich with natural gifts but impoverished in our inner space. We must bring our lives into discipline and remain intentional about the care of our inner self and private world.

[10] Gordon MacDonald. V-XVii
[11] Gordon MacDonald. V-XVii

Coaching Moment:
What can you do to create more harmony between your private and public life?

Don't confuse having a career with having a life
~ Hillary Clinton

May you find the balance of life, time for work but also time for play.
~ Catherine Pulsifer

Work Hard, Play Harder!

All occupations come with occupational hazards. For example, H. B London in his book, *Pastors, An Endangered Species* suggests, that pastors are in danger because of the endless demands of ministry, the unreachable goals that pastors burden themselves with, and the unrealistic expectations of their congregations. Far too many pastors have become routinized in the practice of ministry but have neglected the care of their own souls. Many have become proficient in the pulpit but have become deficient in Christian virtue.

Far too few pastors take seriously the notion of their own emotional, physical and spiritual health. The result of these and other factors have led to an alarming burnout, dropout and moral failure rate among pastors. Clergy is not the only profession that must reckon with occupational hazards. Several professionals are frequently working beyond their limitations. Several are stretched, overloaded and overwhelmed by the demands of the business, ministry or job.

Recent studies on Americans work life reveal that Americans work longer hours than most countries. Statistics show that

Americans citizens work 137 hours per year more than Japan, 260 per year more than the UK and 500 per year more than France.[12] At least 134 countries have laws that regulate the maximum hours its' citizens are allowed to work during the week. However, America has no such laws. In fact, data from the U. S. Bureau of Labor Statistics reveal the following:

- In the United States 85.8% of males and 66.5% of females work more than 40 hours per week.
- The average productivity per American worker has increased 400% since 1950.
- There is not a federal law requiring paid sick days in the United States.
- The U.S. remains the only industrialized country in the world that has no legally mandated annual leave.
- In every country including Canada and Japan, workers get at least 20 paid vacation days. In France and Finland, they get 30 – an entire month off, paid, every year.

American labor trends show that American workers leave more sick time, leave time and vacations on the table at the end of the calendar year. This has resulted in an increase in work related stress and health problems. Additionally, American workers often report having less quality of life, decreased life satisfaction and struggles to find life/work balance or harmony.

Every profession has occupational hazards that we must cleverly avoid to ensure that we do not succumb to its perils. All workers, pastors, police officers, politicians, business owners, corporate executives and employees must recognize their human limitations. The impact of too much work will result in high levels of stress. This will harm our emotional, mental, physical and spiritual well-being.

---

[12]Liz Bagot. Americans Work Harder Than Any Other Countries Citizens. New York Post, September 3, 2017.

A popular slogan encourages people to balance work with play. It says, "Work Hard/Play Hard." I will take it a little further and encourage us to Work Hard/Play Harder! Take yourself back to grade school and watch yourself running around the playground at recess. Remember how it made you feel to be outside experiencing the freedom of the open air. Recess often came in the afternoon after a morning of classroom work. It would often include a snack and it always included other children to play with and enjoy. Like recess, inserting play into our work life, energizes to make it to the end of the work day, week, month and year.

I suggest, it takes twice as much play to balance the effects of hard work. Here are some practical steps you and I can take:
- Discover what you enjoy doing after work.
- Make a commitment to doing what you enjoy after work.
- Spend time with people you enjoy after work.
- Move toward working fewer hours in the week, month and year.
- Take scheduled and spontaneous days off work.
- Take at least 2-4 weeks off work each year. (You will more likely take a week vacation quarterly than entire month.)
- Take your paid leave time.
- Take maternity and paternity leave.
- Take your sick time as needed.
- Take family medical leave as needed.
- Plan and take vacations with your family, friends and alone.
- Do something fun daily, weekly, monthly and yearly.
- Do something fun that reminds you of your childhood recess time.
- Make a date with yourself.
- Keep your date with yourself
- Learn to laugh at yourself and others.
- Work Hard and Play Harder!

Coaching Moment:
Reflect the section above and answer the following questions:

What occupational hazards are associated with your profession? _____
_____
_____
_____
_____
_____

Based upon American labor trends, what new commitments do you need to make in order to bring greater harmony in your life and work?
_____
_____
_____
_____

How can you play harder as it relates to your work?
_____
_____
_____
_____

Where would you like to go on your next vacation?
_____
_____
_____

When will you go?
_____
_____
_____

Like a path through the forest, Sabbath creates a marker for ourselves so, if we are lost, we can find our way back to our center.
~ Wayne Muller

Almost everything will work again if you unplug it for a few minutes, including you.
~ Anne Lamott

Replenish Your Soul with Spiritual Disciplines

One of the greatest commandments in the Bible, is probably one you have heard and it may be one you have quoted, "Thou shall love thy neighbor as thyself." So important is this commandment that it is stated in the Old Testament twice by God to Moses (Leviticus 19:18; 34), repeated several times in the New Testament by Jesus (Matthew 22:39; Mark 12:33; Luke 10:27) and can also be found in the writings of the apostles Paul and James (Romans 13:9; Galatians 5:14; James 2:8). What I find most interesting about this commandment is the ideal that I really can't "love my neighbor" until I "love myself."

Many times we are so busy focusing on the needs of our families, friends and that we fail to replenish our own souls. We make excuses about not having time for ourselves because of the demands of work, school, and professional pursuits. Yet, we are impoverished because we have neglected this vital principle. In order to demonstrate love for others, you must love yourself. In order to replenish others, you must replenish your own soul.

Sabbath-Keeping

Wayne Muller describes Sabbath as complete surrender. He states, "Sabbath is more than the absence of work; it is not just a day off, when we catch up on television or errands. It is the presence of something that arises when we consecrate a period of time to listen to what is most deeply beautiful, nourishing or true.[13] Therefore, Sabbath is uncluttered time and space to distance myself from the frenzied activities of the day and week. It is a time for quieting my internal noises. This uncluttered time and space serves to detach me from external things to which I cling to for my identity. Sabbath gives me the opportunity to offer these things back to God in rest and reflection.

Retreat

In scripture we often find Jesus feeding the multitudes, preaching in the synagogues, teaching on the mountains and healing all manner of sickness and disease. All this is true of Jesus and His ministry. However, as often as you saw Jesus doing these things, you also saw him retreating, sending the people away, or disappearing without a warning. Jesus would often retreat to a special place of rest (see Matthew 14:23; Luke 5:15-16; Mark 1:32-33). Jesus did not wait until everyone had been properly cared for or until all who sought him were healed. He did not seek the opinion or permission of others when he felt the need to pull away and he did feel the need to inform his closets disciples concerning where he was going. Wayne Muller says, "Jesus obeyed a deeper rhythm. When the moment of rest had come, the time for healing was over. He would simply stop, retire to a quiet place, and pray."[14]

---

[13]Wayne Muller; 8.

[14]Wayne Muller; 25.

Prayer

Prayer is one of the keys to unlocking God's heart and releasing the potential and the desires of our own hearts is prayer. Prayer is the act in which I bring myself to attention before God. Through prayer we are privileged to encounter the Spirit of God. Prayer evokes in us a desire to conform into the image that God has designed for us rather than perform for the acceptance and the applause of men. Through prayer our focus is redirected away from perfection and away from those emotions and habits that control us by trying to measure up to some external, idealized standard.

Lectio Divina

This form of spiritual reading is accomplished through the reading of biblical texts and other holy texts. It is an approach to the scriptures that requires an intentional listening as the scripture becomes a transforming encounter.[15]

Silence and Solitude

To be silent means to refrain from talking, to refrain from paying attention to the sounds around us. Learn to disconnect by to turning off the television, the radio, the CD player, and social media. The goal of silence is to seek a quiet place for paying attention to God and the thoughts of your own mind.

Reflection

One of the primary benefits of Sabbath keeping is that it allows time for reflection. Reflection is a very enlightening experience as we think about and process our experiences to find meaning and purpose.

---

[15]Robert Mullholland. Invitation to a Journey. Downers Grove, IL: InterVarsity Press 1993.

Journaling
Written thoughts and daily, monthly, yearly recording of personal experiences. This is done with the purpose of reflecting and capturing insights and lessons learned throughout one's life.

Fasting
Fasting is abstinence from food, or certain types of food as an act of sacrifice and spiritual renewal or religious observance.

Doing Nothing
David Kundtz in the book Stopping, defines 'doing nothing' in relative terms. He says "Sometimes it means not doing too much, doing something that takes very little energy, or doing something that you love to do. In other words, it's relative and it's paradoxical because 'doing nothing' can be beneficial." [16]

Stop
Kundtz suggests, we can take 'Stopping' moments in one of three ways: Stillpoints, Stopovers, or Grinding Halts.[17] Stillpoints are the "heart and soul of stopping. These are intentional breaks or breathers in our day such as:

- Bathroom breather: one of the best places to go for a Stillpoint.
- A scheduled break.
- Walking from one task to another.
- The commute home gives time to decompress by putting on music, and beginning the process focusing your mind away from work and toward your home, family and the things you enjoy.

---

[16]David Kundtz. Stopping: How to be Still When You Have to Keep Going. Berkeley, CA: Conari Press, 1998, 13-16.

[17]David Kundtz. 57-72.

Stopovers are short stops that only take a few days or a weekend getaway. Kundtz purports that it is more likely that we will take a full day off every two months for a Stopover than we are to take an hour every day for meditation.[18] Both are good he says, but the question is which will you actually do?

Examples:
- A structured weekend retreat.
- Create your own or personal retreat.
- A bus trip or train ride.
- An overnight stay.
- Just staying home or pajama day.
- A spontaneous opportunity when all of a sudden some space has been created in your day, an appointment is canceled, the kids are in school, your husband is out of town. You didn't plan and God gives you this window of opportunity to rest.
- A birthday gift to yourself – spa, lunch, dinner, something you have desired, a message to yourself, a card, buying fresh flowers, candles, etc.
- A day off work for rest and rejuvenation.

Grinding Halts indicate that something big is about to happen or change. They are often needed to avoid some undesired result. For example: I need to stop to pay attention to my marriage, children, health. God is changing my direction. The course of my life is going in a new direction such as a career change, change in marital status, change in family structure requiring a change in the way I operate and function in the world.[19]

---

[18] David Kundtz. 73-96

[19] David Kundtz. 97-104

Examples:
- Extended Personal Spiritual Retreat (1-2 weeks)
- Time alone in the mountains or a secluded space.
- Illness or major surgery.
- The death of a loved one or a divorce.
- Sabbatical: A year or time period off of work for rest, reflection and renewal.

Coaching Moment:
Which of these replenishing self-care practices have you experienced? Reflect on the results of your experiences? Which of these self-care practices would you like to explore? Why? When?

Self-care is never a selfish act - it is simply good stewardship of the only gift I have, the gift I was put on earth to offer others. Anytime we can listen to true self and give the care it requires, we do it not only for ourselves, but for the many others whose lives we touch.
~ Parker J. Palmer

Create Your Self-Care Board of Directors

Living a lifestyle of harmony requires that we engage, consult and inquire of persons with varied skill sets and expertise to which we can draw encouragement, information, inspiration, insight and instruction. I call these people my, Self-Care Board of Directors. These are the persons to whom I have made myself accountable for living a healthy, holistic lifestyle of harmony. Below are some people groups and professionals you should consider adding to your Self-Care Board of Directors. Having such people in your life will aid you in living an integrated life of wholeness and enhance your self-care journey.

Family and Friends
Family members and friends are key players on your self-care board of directors. Find creative ways to involve your family and friends in your self-care plans. For example:
- Find healthy recipes to cook and eat healthy meals together.
- Discover physical activities that you can do as a group or team, such as bike riding, hiking, swimming, etc.
- Talk through schedules and commitments and make the necessary adjustments to support one another's self-care goals, needs and plans.

Medical Professionals
Maintaining relationships with medical professionals for routine check-ups, medical exams and screenings are vital to self-care. Keeping healthy blood pressure, cholesterol and blood sugar levels are extremely important. Good oral hygiene is also vital to your medical health. Practice good oral hygiene with regular dental and periodontal visits and make necessary corrections to any dental and periodontal concerns. Knowing your body is important as well. For example, when I noticed my heart racing and rapid weight loss, I immediately consulted my primary care physician and followed up on his referral to see an endocrinologist. If you have specific health concerns, seek the aide of specific specialists such as cardiologists, gynecologists, rheumatologists, chiropractor or other specialists who will assist you maintaining excellent physical health.

Mental Health Counselors, Therapists and Psychiatrists
Mental health treatment and therapy is a critical factor in self-care. Many mental disorders such as anxiety disorders, clinical depression, mood disorders, bipolar disorders, dementia, attention deficit, hyperactivity and schizophrenia can cause negative impact on your physical and mental health. There are societal, cultural and familial stigmas that prevent people from seeking the help of mental health professionals. However, we must help ourselves and others overcome such stigmas. Seeking the advice and counsel of mental health professionals will greatly benefit us in processing our life experiences and assist in the development of strategies for treatment, supervision and resolutions to mental health challenges.

Nutritionists & Healthy Eating Coaches
A nutritionist is a person who advises on matters of food, nutrition and healthy eating. These healthy eating coaches can help us identify the foods that are necessary for specific bodily functions. Consulting a nutritionist or dietician can aid in the development of proper eating habits, patterns and routines. Nutrition-

ists and healthy eating coaches also provide emotional support for healthy weight goals and creativity with meal preparation.

Personal Trainers & Fitness Coaches
A personal trainer is an individual certified with varying degrees of knowledge related to general fitness. This knowledge includes exercise instruction and routines. Personal trainers or fitness coaches assist and motivate clients in setting and reaching physical fitness goals. They provide feedback, support and accountability. I highly recommend personal trainers and fitness coaches in creating harmony and maintaining self-care.

Life Coaches
Life coaches are persons who specialize in providing the help necessary to move people forward in setting personal and professional goals that bring purpose and significance in their lives. Most life coaching clients are people who might find themselves successful in many areas but stuck in other areas of their lives. Coaching clients may also be people who desire to make change in their personal lives and want the support of a life coach. I describe coaching relationships as a co-active relationship where a coach offers the support, encouragement and accountability that is necessary for you to live your best life!

Spiritual Directors
Spiritual direction is the practice of being with people as they attempt to deepen their relationship with the divine, or to learn and grow in their own personal spirituality. "The whole purpose of spiritual direction is to penetrate beneath the surface of a person's life, to get behind the facade of conventional gestures and attitudes which one presents to the world, and to bring out one's inner spiritual freedom, one's inmost truth, which is what Christians call the likeness of Christ in one's soul." Thomas Merton, Trappist Monk, USA.

Coaching Moment:

Which of the above listed above do you have on your self-care board of directors? Which of the listed above do you need to onboard? How would your life improve if you added one or more of these persons to your self-care board of directors?

*Do not be afraid to ask for help. There is no shame.
It's not too private. Don't be too prideful. Remember, in this very moment, you are
trapped in your knowledge, understanding, and insights. By sharing and
seeking help from another, you may gain new knowledge, understanding, and insights.
This can bring you leaps and bounds forward. Reach out to a trusted friend,
to a group, or a therapist. What if you can
improve your life, the quality of your life? What if you have that chance?
Isn't it worth it to try?*
~ Akiroq Brost

Develop Your Self-Care Plan

I invite you into a journey of self-care that is governed by a synchronized rhythm of work and rest. This journey will take courage on your part. It may be a lonesome journey at times but with the right people on the path you are guaranteed a life of harmony. Take a few moments to review the way you answered the coaching questions in the previous chapters and develop your self-care plan.

Remember your plan must be consistent with who you are, what you enjoy, your values and your specific life circumstances. Do not be intimidated by what others around you are doing. Do not be afraid to try new adventures and creative strategies to enhance your experiences. Go inward, be intentional and balance your work with play. Engage in spiritual and disciplines and make sure you onboard the right people.

This is your self-care plan so I will not presume to write it for you. Feel free to use the following blank pages or grab your favorite notebook and begin writing. Happy writing, blessed living and may your life be ever lived in harmony….

My Self Care-Plan

My Self Care-Plan

My Self Care-Plan

My Self Care-Plan

My Self Care-Plan

My Self Care-Plan

Self-Care Quotes

"Do something every day that is loving toward your body and gives you the opportunity to enjoy the sensations of your body."
~Golda Poretsky

"There are days I drop words of comfort on myself like falling leaves and remember that it is enough to be taken care of by myself."
~ Brian Andreas

"Your breathing is your greatest friend. Return to it in all your troubles and you will find comfort and guidance."
~ Unknown

"When the well's dry, we know the worth of water."
~ Benjamin Franklin

"Our bodies are our gardens to which our wills are gardeners."
~ William Shakespeare

"Don't sacrifice yourself too much, because if you sacrifice too much there's nothing else you can give and nobody will care for you."
~ Karl Lagerfeld

"The thing that is really hard, and really amazing, is giving up on being perfect and beginning the work of becoming yourself."
~ Anna Quindlen

"Self-compassion is simply giving the same kindness to ourselves that we would give to others."
~ Christopher Germer

"People who love themselves come across as very loving, generous and kind; they express their self-confidence through humility, forgiveness and inclusiveness."
~ Sanaya Roman

"When we give ourselves compassion, we are opening our hearts in a way that can transform our lives."
~ Kristin Neff

"Solitude is where I place my chaos to rest and awaken my inner peace."
~ Nikki Rowe

"Time you enjoy wasting is not wasted time."
~ Unknown

"Those who think they have not time for bodily exercise will sooner or later have to find time for illness."
~ Edward Stanley

"Sometimes the most important thing in a whole day is the rest we take between two deep breaths."
~ Etty Hillesum

"Knowing how to be solitary is central to the art of loving. When we can be alone, we can be with others without using them as a means of escape."
~ bell hooks

"Be you, love you. All ways, always."
~ Alexandra Elle

"If we only stop when we are finished with all our work, we will never stop, because our work is never completely done. With every accomplishment there arises a new responsibility. Sabbath dissolves the artificial urgency of our days, because it liberates us from the need to be finished."
~ Wayne Muller

Walking is the best possible exercise. Habituate yourself to walk very far.
~ Thomas Jefferson

The reason I exercise is for the quality of life I enjoy.
~ Kenneth H. Cooper

It's not enough to be busy, so are the ants. The question is, what are we busy about?
~ Henry David Thoreau

He lives long that lives well; and time misspent is not lived but lost.
~ Thomas Fuller

Time is the most valuable thing a man can spend.
~ Theophrastus

Money, I can only gain or lose. But time I can only lose. So, I must spend it carefully.
~ Unknown

Your life is a statement to the world representing your values, your beliefs, your dreams.
~ David Areson

Recommended Reading List

Blackaby, Henry & Richard (2001). Spiritual Leadership. Nashville, TN: Broadman & Holman Publishers.

Benson, Bob, Sr. and Michael W. Benson. Disciplines for The Inner Life. Nashville: Thomas Nelson, 1989.

Boa, Kenneth. Face to Face: Praying The Scriptures for Spiritual Growth. Grand Rapids: Zondervan, 1997.

Bridges, Jerry. The Practices of Godliness. Colorado Springs: NavPress, 1993.

Bridges, Jerry. The Practices of Goodness. Colorado Springs: NavPress, 1997.

Bridges, Jerry. The Pursuit of Holiness. Colorado Springs: NavPress, 1996.

Cashman, Kevin. Leadership from The Inside Out. Minneapolis: Leader Source, 1998.

Chan, Simon. Spiritual Theology: A Systematic Study of the Christian Life. Downers Grove: InterVarsity Press, 1998.

Clinton, J. Robert. The Making of a Leader. Colorado Springs: NavPress, 1988.

Crabb, Larry. Connecting: A Radical New Vision. Nashville: Word Publishing, 1997.

Crabb, Larry. Moving Through Your Problems Toward Finding God. Grand Rapids: Zondervan Publishing House, 1993.

Crabb, Larry. The Safest Place On Earth. Nashville: Thomas Nelson, 1999.

Cordeiro, Wayne. Leading on Empty. Minneapolis: Bethany House, 2009

Edwards, Tidden. Sabbath Time. Nashville: Upper Room, 1992.

Elliff, Tom. A Passion for Prayer. Wheaton, IL: Crossway Books, 1998.

Foster, Richard J. Devotional Classics: Selected Readings for Individuals and Groups. San Francisco: Harper, 1993.

Foster, Richard J. Celebration of Discipline: The Path to Spiritual Growth. San Francisco: Harper, 1988.

Hybels, Bill. Too Busy Not to Pray. Downer Grove, IL: InterVarsity Press, 1998.

Job, Rueben P. A Guide to Retreat For All God's Shepherds. Nashville: Abingdon Press, 1994.

Kundtz, David. Stopping: How To Be Still When You Have To Keep Going. Berkeley: Conari Press, 1998.

Klug, Ronald. How To Keep a Spiritual Journal. Minneapolis: Augsburg, 1993.

Lewis, Phillip V. Transformational Leadership: A New Model for Total Church Involvement. Nashville: Broadman & Holman Publishers, 1996.

MacDonald, Gordon. Ordering Your Private World. Nashville, TN: Thomas Nelson, Inc. 2003.

Mulholland, M. Robert. Invitation To A Journey. Downers Grove, IL: InterVarsity Press 1993.

Muller, Wayne. Sabbath: Finding Rest, Renewal and Delight in Our Daily Lives. New York: Bantam Books, 1999

Peterson, Eugene. Working the Angles: The Shape of Pastoral Integrity. Grand Rapids: William B Eerdmans Publishing, 1987.

Reccord, Bob. Forged by Fire: How God Shapes Those He Loves. Nashville: Broadman & Holman Publishers, 2000.

Scazzero, Peter. The Emotionally Healthy Church. Grand Rapids: Zondervan, 2003.

Spurgeon, Charles. The Power of Prayer in a Believer's Life. Lynwood, WA: Emerald Books, 1993.

Thielen, Martin. Searching for Happiness. How Generosity, Faith and Other Spiritual Habits Can Lead to a Full Life. Louisville: Westminster John Knox Press, 2016.